Yucky Food

by
Helen and Sarah Orme

The de Ferrers Academy
St Mary's Drive
Burton on Trent
DE13 0LL

Thunderbolts

Yucky Food
by Helen and Sarah Orme

Illustrated by Jacqui Clark

Published by Ransom Publishing Ltd.
Radley House, 8 St. Cross Road, Winchester, Hants. SO23 9HX, UK
www.ransom.co.uk

ISBN   978 178127 079 0
First published in 2013
Copyright © 2013 Ransom Publishing Ltd.

Illustrations copyright © 2013 Jacqui Clark
'Get the Facts' section - images copyright: cover, prelims, passim – An-d, istolethetv, Thomas Schoch; pp 4/5 - istolethetv; pp 6/7 - Holger Mette, Alan Wilson, Greg Hume, Kevin Walsh, Ron Hohenhaus, fir0002/flagstaffotos.com.au; pp 8/9 - Einsamer Schütze, MarcusObal; pp 10/11 - Pavlo Lutsan, Richard Bartz, Jerzy Strzelecki; pp 12/13 - Dmitriy Berkut, Paweł Drozd, Pangamut; pp 14/15 - Håkan Svensson, Jürgen Howaldt; pp 16/17 - Helen Orme, Richard Loader; pp 18/19 - An-d, Thomas Schoch; pp 20/21 - ronnieliew, Shardan, Serenity, Stu Spivack, TigrouMeow; pp 22/23 - Helen Orme, -Oxford-; p 36 - Mat Connolley.

A CIP catalogue record of this book is available from the British Library.

All rights reserved. No part of this publication may be reproduced, stored in a retrieval system, or transmitted, in any form or by any means, electronic, mechanical, photocopying, recording or otherwise, without the prior permission of the publishers.

The rights of Helen and Sarah Orme to be identified as the authors and of Jacqui Clark to be identified as the illustrator of this Work have been asserted by them in accordance with sections 77 and 78 of the Copyright, Design and Patents Act 1988.

Contents

Yucky Food: The Facts — 5

1	Some people like it	6
2	Prehistoric food	8
3	Roman food	10
4	Deadly food!	12
5	Really wild food	14
6	Wild food at home	16
7	Yummy insects!	18
8	The world's yuckiest food?	20
9	Looks yucky – tastes great!	22

Top Cooks! — 25

Yucky Food: The Facts

Some people like it

People from different parts of the world eat different food.

In the past, people could only eat the food that came from where they lived.

Who ate these foods?

1

2

All change:

Around the world, people are changing what they eat.

They can eat food that comes from other countries. They are eating more processed food.

Are they healthier?

Not always!

Answers: 1 – Inuit from Canada.
2 – Aboriginal people from Australia.

Prehistoric food

Prehistoric people collected food such as nuts and seeds. They also hunted for meat.

Two important discoveries:

Fire

Fire meant you could cook food properly rather than eat it raw. This was easier to digest and tasted much better!

Pottery

Pottery meant that you could stew and boil food – a much better way to cook it.

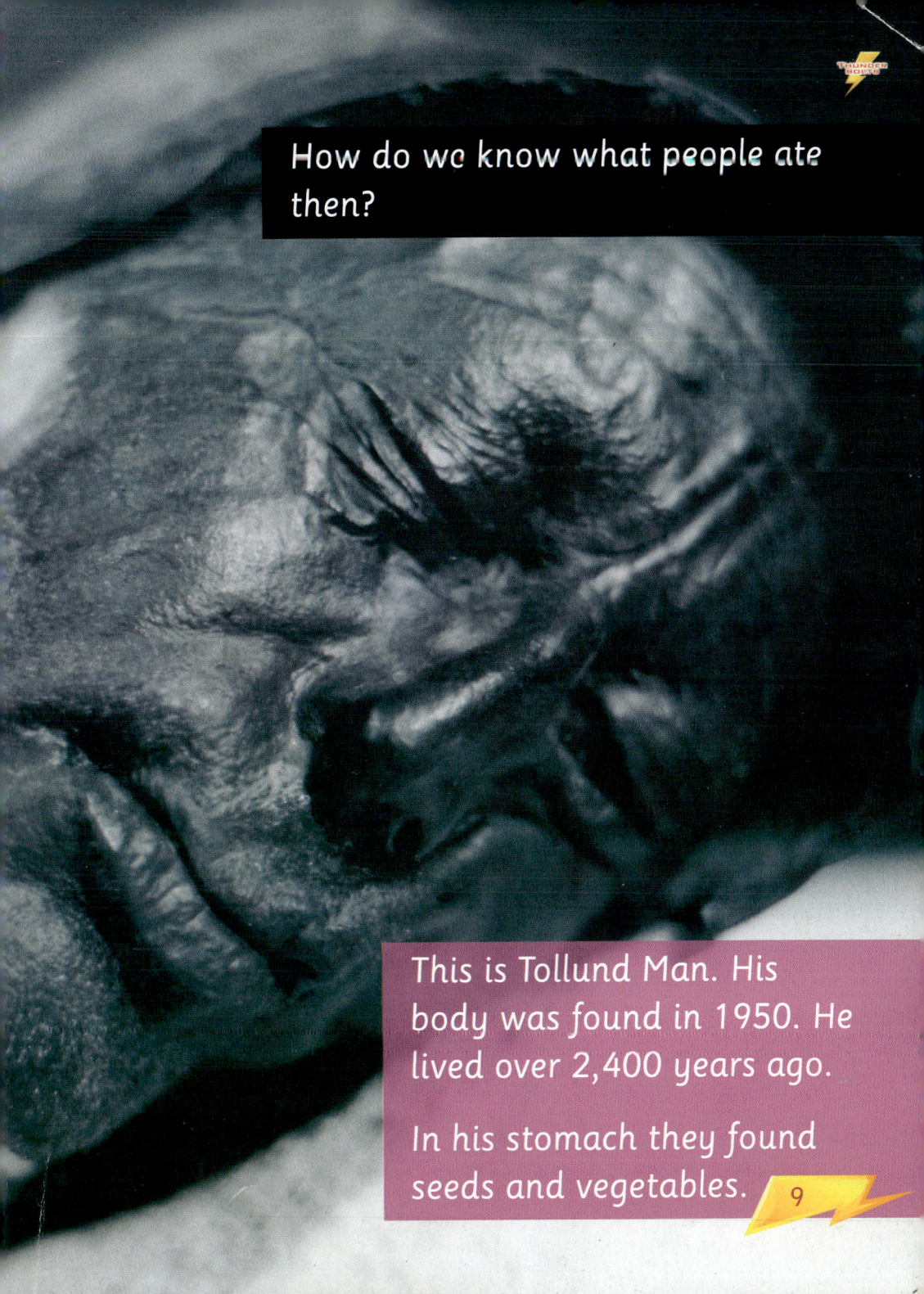

How do we know what people ate then?

This is Tollund Man. His body was found in 1950. He lived over 2,400 years ago.

In his stomach they found seeds and vegetables.

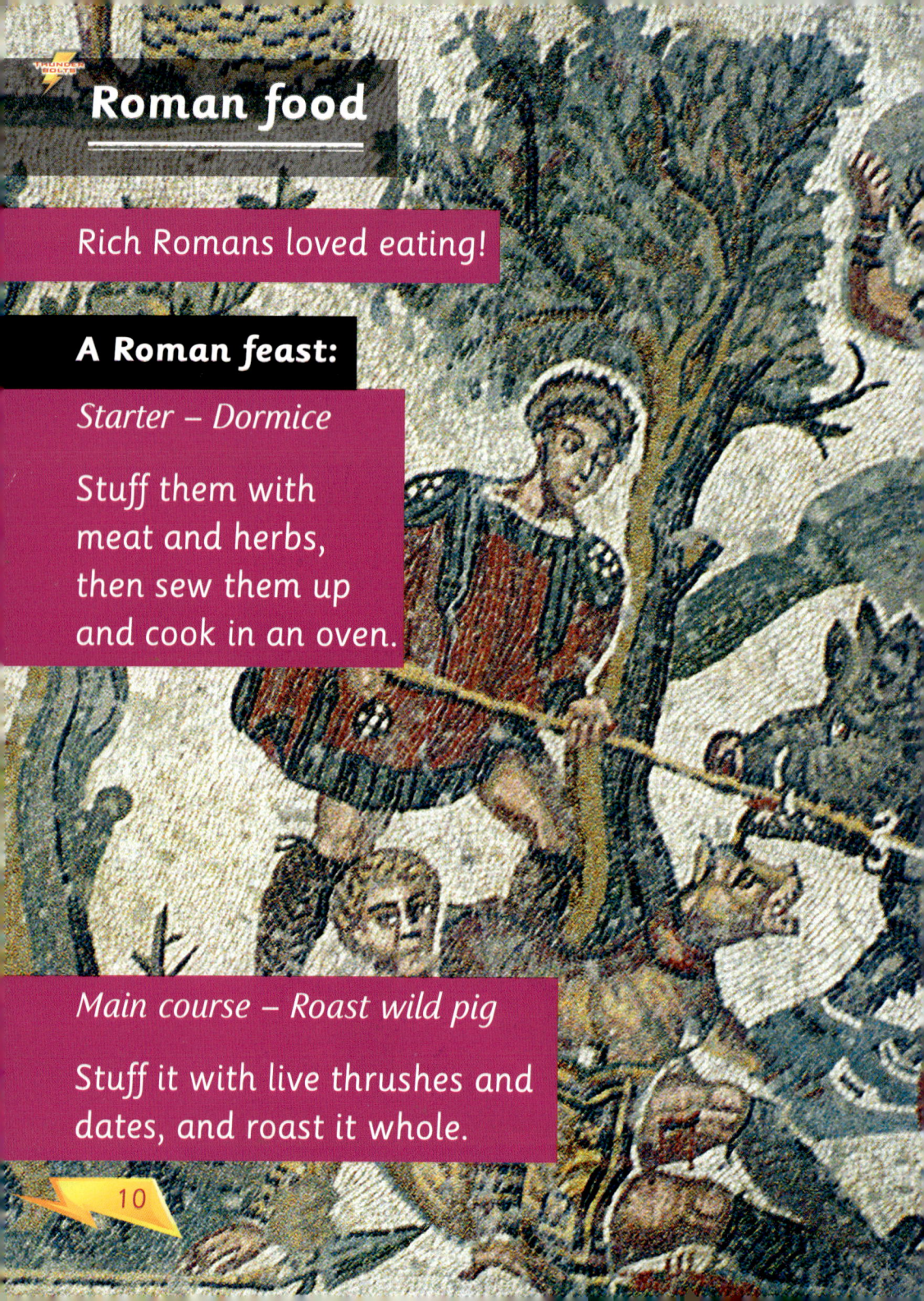

Roman food

Rich Romans loved eating!

A Roman feast:

Starter – Dormice

Stuff them with meat and herbs, then sew them up and cook in an oven.

Main course – Roast wild pig

Stuff it with live thrushes and dates, and roast it whole.

Starter

Main course

Then what?

They would go out to be sick. Then start eating all over again!

Deadly food!

This fish is called a fugu.

Japanese people love to eat it. They say it's delicious!

But parts of it are so poisonous it can kill you.

You need to be very well trained to cook fugu!

Fugu ready to eat.

If food isn't made properly, it can make you ill.

In some parts of the world, meat can have small eggs in it.

These can grow inside your body if the meat isn't cooked properly.

These are worms inside someone's body. Yuk!

Really wild food

Do you really need to go shopping?

There are things all around you that you can eat – but you may not want to!

Slugs

How to cook them:

Give them a good clean to get rid of the slime. Then cook them in tomato sauce.

Hedgehogs

Cover them with clay, then roast them. Take the prickles off before you eat it!

Wild food at home

Here is one you *can* try at home. Nettle soup: it won't sting you and it tastes great!

What you need:

- A bowl full of nettles
- 2 tablespoons cooking oil
- 1 medium onion
- 1 large potato
- 1 litre of vegetable stock
- Salt.

What to do:

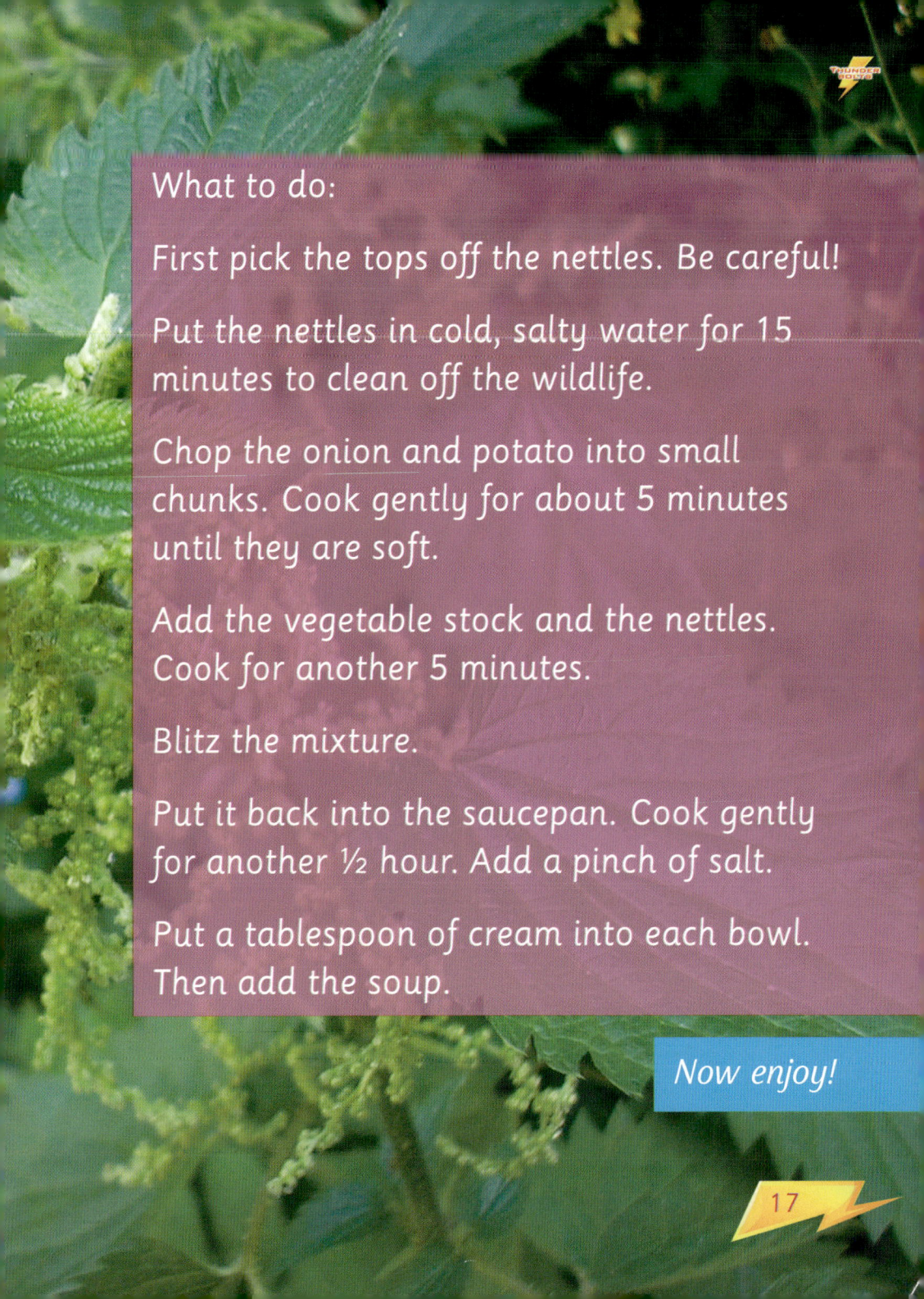

First pick the tops off the nettles. Be careful!

Put the nettles in cold, salty water for 15 minutes to clean off the wildlife.

Chop the onion and potato into small chunks. Cook gently for about 5 minutes until they are soft.

Add the vegetable stock and the nettles. Cook for another 5 minutes.

Blitz the mixture.

Put it back into the saucepan. Cook gently for another ½ hour. Add a pinch of salt.

Put a tablespoon of cream into each bowl. Then add the soup.

Now enjoy!

Yummy insects!

Crunchy cockroaches? Munchy maggots? Tasty tarantulas?

Does this sound yucky?

Well, some people think that insects and spiders are the food of the future!

Why?

Using insects for food is better for the planet. Animals like cows and chickens need lots of food to grow. Insects need much less to make the same amount of food for us.

Plenty of insects are already eaten around the world. People say they taste really good!

Why not try:

- Cockroach curry
- Grasshopper tacos
- Fish in wood-louse sauce
- Chocolate scorpions
- Deep-fried dung beetles.

Deep-fried tarantula: a quick snack!

The world's yuckiest food?

Maggoty cheese. This is eaten in Italy.

Do you eat the maggots as well as the cheese? Some people do – but only if the maggots are still alive.

Eyeball soup.

Where do the eyeballs come from? Sheep.

What does it taste like? Nice and chewy!

Birds Nest soup.

That doesn't sound too bad. What's it really made of?

Bird spit.

Civet cat coffee.

What is it made of? Coffee beans.

But the civet cat (that's this little guy, below) eats them first. The beans are then collected from the animal's poo.

Would you like a cup?

Main picture: coffee beans – *after* the civet cat has eaten them.

Looks yucky – tastes great!

In the story that follows, Sarah makes spicy chicken. It looks yucky – but tastes great!

You could try this recipe at home. You will need:

- 4 chicken portions, and these things to make the sauce:

- 1 tablespoon of vegetable oil
- 2 tablespoons of soy sauce
- 1 tablespoon of honey
- 1 tablespoon of tomato purée
- ½ teaspoon hot pepper sauce.

Before cooking

Put all the sauce ingredients into a bowl and mix well. Cover the chicken portions with the sauce.

Leave in the fridge for 1 hour.

Heat the oven to 200°C – Gas Mark 6.

Pour the rest of the sauce over the chicken pieces. Add 2 tablespoons of water.

Cover the chicken and cook for about 30 minutes.

Take the chicken out of the oven.

Important: check it is cooked. You may need an adult helper for this.

After cooking

Yummy!

Top Cooks! 1

Kate and Sarah loved TV cooking shows!

They decided to do one of their own, for their family. Sarah was going to cook the main course, and Kate would make the pudding.

The rest of the family would judge which was best.

Top Cooks! 2

Sarah decided to make spicy chicken.

She got lots of spices out of the cupboard and mixed them up. Then she covered the chicken pieces with the spices and put them in the oven.

Kate went into the garden to pick some fruit.

Top Cooks!

Kate had decided to make pancakes.

When they were done, she got some cream out of the fridge and poured it over the pancakes. Then she put the fruit on top.

She thought they looked great!

Top Cooks!

It was time to serve the meal. The whole family was waiting at the table.

Sarah brought out the chicken. It didn't look good! Will said that Sarah must have burnt it.

When Kate brought the pancakes in, they were all sure she would win!

Top Cooks!   5

Sarah served up the chicken and Dad put some in his mouth.

'Wow' was all he said.

Everyone else tried it. They loved it.

Will looked at his pancake. Something was moving on it! It was greenfly from the garden!

The winner was Sarah!

Word list

The de Ferrers Academy
St Mary's Drive
Burton on Trent
DE13 0LL

Aboriginal
Australia
blitz
civet cat
cockroach
country
deadly
different
eyeball
fugu
healthier
hedgehog
ingredients
Inuit
litre
onion
poisonous
potato
pottery
prehistoric
processed
purée
raspberries
Roman
saucepan
soy
spice
stew
stomach
tacos
tarantula
Tollund Man
tomato
vegetable